Introduction

In its time, Hilsea Lido has linked exotic architecture with sport, fashion, film, music and dance, body-building and physical culture, and most of all, lots of fun in sparkling blue water.

Designed by the City Engineer, Joseph Parkin and opened officially by the Lord Mayor of the City of Portsmouth, Councillor Frank J. Privett, J.P. on 24 July 1935, its Art Deco architecture brought the stylish sophistication of the 1930's Lido lifestyle to Portsmouth for the first time. The main pool became the setting for the fashionable outfits and accessories of the day - the place to see and be seen.

The pool was also designed to make the most of the Thirties' enthusiasm for fresh air and organised physical culture. It formed the backdrop to swimming and diving competitions, water polo, aquatic galas, novelty events and re-enactments of Naval battles using model boats.

Hilsea Lido 75 gives us a chance to enjoy a pleasurable and nostalgic trip back over the last 75 years and, in the process, gives us a glimpse of the vitality and excitement that was Lido life. This booklet also includes postcards and photographs evoking memories of the important role that Hilsea Lido played and still plays in the lives of generations of local people.

My thanks go to Dianne Bennett of First Fitness; Mark Clowes; Cllr. Terry Hall; Lauren Hill; Larry Hudson; Janis Loose; Olive Steggall; Alan King of the Norrish Central Library, Portsmouth; John Stedman of Portsmouth City Museum; Gail, Dan and Eve McGovren of 131 Design; Lee Asher and Laura Jones of Prontaprint; The News and the Robert Stigwood Organisation for all their help in putting this booklet together.

Lastly, my thanks as always, go to the people of Hilsea. It has been a privilege to work with them on this important anniversary and without them, this booklet would not have been possible.

Jane Smith,
Southsea,
May 2010.

"...A fine City achievement................."

The opening ceremony at the main pool on 24 July 2010. The Lord Mayor (standing) can be seen on the left. *(Courtesy of The News)*

The Lord Mayor unveiled this plaque which can just be seen under the centre window of the small spectator stand on the far right hand side. The plaque was removed during a refurbishment in the 1960s and never replaced. Unseen for 30 years it was re-discovered in 1995 and given to Portsmouth City Museum.

"…When are the dignitaries going to stop talking?!!………"

The late Joyce Arnett (left) with her sister Olive Steggall on 24 July 1985
(Courtesy of The News)

Olive Steggall today

Olive Steggall of Hilsea was present at the opening ceremony in 1935 aged nine but outside! Local people were not admitted to the pool until the formalities had been concluded and in the photograph of the opening can be seen watching from behind the gates.

Now one of the few survivors of an older generation whose memories span 75 years, she recalls, "…we were all there at the back…lined up in our bathers…all we could think about, jumping up and down, was when they were going to stop talking and we could get in the pool. I'm sure it was a nice day but I wasn't interested in the dignitaries…!"

The photograph above shows Olive and her sister Joyce at the Lido's Golden Anniversary. All swimmers were charged 1935 entry prices, 2p (6d) for adults and 1p (3d) for children.

Great Times at Hilsea Lido

24 August 1936 *(Courtesy of The News)*

Gala Fun at the Lido

12 August 1935 *(Courtesy of The News)*

Lively shots of fun at the Lido have always been a great favourite with The News. These four captions say it all! They would be repeated many times over the coming years.

The latest fashion in Lido swim wear during the pre-War seasons were one-piece costumes for both boys and girls, probably knitted, and plain swimming hats. As for spectators, the ladies wore summer dresses and sunhats and the gentlemen, blazers and smart trilbies.

Keeping cool on the hottest day of the year, 2 August 1938 *(Courtesy of The News)*

Making a splash at the Hilsea Lido

11 September 1938
(Courtesy of The News)

The Lido Lifestyle..................

The Lido deck of a 1930s luxury ocean-going liner….or is it? The main pool shown here in its first season carries a resonance of the large liner with its rows of windows, the sun deck and its little "bridge", all set off by the lady next to the cascade dressed in the last word in stylish cruise wear.

Basic fashion accessories were also influenced by the Lido style - here's a brooch in the shape of a racquet and ball made in the new material of plastic. Even the lowly hair grip can acquire the glamour of the Lido.

A swimsuit dated 28 August 1926 modelled by Eve McGovren. *(Courtesy of Janis Loose.)*

Clarice Cliff (1899-1972), the famous ceramic designer, produced her Lido Lady in 1931/32. Smoking was considered to be the height of sophistication in the Thirties so its accessory, the ash-tray, was combined with the lady in her elegant beach pyjamas to make the latest in decorative ceramics. This is a reproduction issued by the Clarice Cliff Club as part of their 1999 Centenary year ware.
(Courtesy of the Clarice Cliff Club.)

This entrance arch and tower to Hilsea Lido makes the entry to the site look most inviting but it was also an example of the cutting edge of design in 1938. Designed by the new City Architect Adrien Sharp, it was influenced by the tower at Lee-on-the-Solent (1935) and the tower in the Glasgow Empire Exhibition (1938). All three illustrated the American Art Deco Streamline style which derived originally from New York skyscrapers. We can also detect here a resonance of the ship's funnel to match the nautical features of the main pool further on. The Hilsea arch and tower was demolished in 1968 to make way for the widening of the London Road and extending of the Portsbridge roundabout. The tower at Lee was demolished in 1971.
(Courtesy of Portsmouth City Museums and Records Service.)

Wish You Were Here.......

Over 60 postcards have been produced of the Lido in its 75 years. Here's a selection showing lovely views of the site itself, the main pool, the children's paddling pool and that special favourite, the miniature railway. The voices from the past speak to us from the messages on the back bringing the views alive…

Postmarked 20 May 1937:
"…We had a splendid view from the window yesterday. The King, Queen and Princess Elizabeth drove slowly passed in an open car. Other cars following were closed…"
Note: King George VI, the late Queen Mother and Princess Elizabeth (now Queen Elizabeth II) visited Portsmouth for the Coronation Fleet Review at Spithead on 20 May 1937. 141 Royal Naval ships took part in what was to be the last peacetime Naval event of the 1930s.

No date:
"…Dear Esme,
Here is the pool in full swing. The people are flocking past here. Now it is 12 midday and the weather is fine….Uncle"

Postmarked 22 July 1953:
"…Tuesday 21st, we have just had a swim in this pool…."

Postmarked 11 August 1936:
"….We are having lovely weather. I was down at this place on Sunday, such a lovely place I wish you were here. This is a bathing pool for children and v. pretty parks close by.."

Postmarked 10 September 1947:
"…This is a nice place for the kiddies…been out trying to get some curtains but no luck…."

Postmarked 2 August 1948:
"Dear Keith,
This is what I have been doing this morning riding on the train on this postcard wish you were here to go too,
Love from Ken xxx"

Dancing Their Way To Health

The Women's League of Health and Beauty was founded in 1930. Its philosophy of health in mind, body and spirit was set out in a book by the founder, Mollie Bagot Stack entitled, "Building the Body Beautiful" (1931). Its motto was "Life is Movement", and its badge shown here illustrates one of its members in a famous leap.

The League was famous for displays of synchronised musical exercises by hundreds of women often outdoors. The Portsmouth Dancing to Health League was an offshoot founded in 1931 and had 1700 members pre-War. Their displays at Portsmouth Guildhall, Fratton Park and Southsea Common were very popular. Here, a smaller contingent go through their routine at the Lido's main pool, all wearing similar athletic-style outfits typical of the League and reported by The News on 16 July 1936.
(Courtesy of The News.)

Besides physical culture, body building was very popular in the 1930s. Bob Woolger founded Britain's first health club in 1931 and contributed trophies to many local sporting events including this aquatic gala at the Lido advertised on 7 July 1938. *(Courtesy of The News.)*

HILSEA SWIMMING POOL
SATURDAY AT 3 p.m.
Great Attraction!!
AQUATIC GALA
INCLUDING
DIVING CHAMPIONSHIPS OF HAMPSHIRE.
1 MEN'S, 2 WOMEN'S, 3, GIRLS'.
'WOOLGAR' SWIMMING CHALLENGE CUP.
RELAY RACES.
PORTSMOUTH SCHOOLS' TEAM CHAMPIONSHIPS
POLO MATCH.
NORTHSEA S.C. (Portsmouth) v. PIRELLI GENERAL S.C. (Southampton).
SOME OF THE FINEST DIVERS IN THE COUNTY WILL PARTICIPATE
ADMISSION ... ... 6d.

The club in Southsea is now known as First Fitness and is run by his daughter Dianne Bennett. Here she is today in the museum dedicated to Arnold Schwarzenegger who trained at the club in the 1960s.
(Courtesy of Dianne Bennett.)